LEADERSHIP AND PEOPLE MANAGEMENT

SHISHIRA SRINIVASA

This book is dedicated to all those people who find it difficult to manage human beings at work place and struggling with conflict at workplace.

Contents

Foreword

" Good teams incorporate teamwork into their culture, creating the building blocks for success."

Preface

Learn to be a better manager by developing leadership and communication skills designed to turn first time managers into great team leaders.

Acknowledgements

I hereby thank the almighty for always being with me in all my endeavours.

I thank my parents for always being supportive and I thank my PhD Guide who has always inspired me to be exceptional in my work.

I thank the readers who are always supportive of my works.

Prologue

Effective people management is a necessary quality for current and aspiring leaders who aim to improve workplace communication and prepare employees for success. Examining the skills that make up people management can help you discover your strengths and identify areas for improvement.

CHAPTER ONE

Managing people

Managing people isnt an easy task

It's not always the case that Employees are a company's most important resource.

Management is essentially the act of supervising and coordinating people and resources to achieve a goal. It's part science, part art form, focusing on areas such as leadership, motivation, planning, and decision-making.

Being a manager is about using your available resources to work towards a common objective. And, as we explore in our ExpertTrack from Savoir-Relier, there are many different management and leadership styles you can use to achieve these goals.

What are management behaviours?

Management behaviours are the actions and traits that make a manager successful. These behaviours, when demonstrated consistently, can help managers bring out the best in the people they're responsible for.

When it comes to managing people effectively, the right actions and strategies can be hugely beneficial to all involved. Whether you're managing one other person or a whole team or organisation, developing the right behaviours can set you up for success.

The first step is to identify the behaviours that bring out the best in others. You can approach this by thinking about the people who have successfully managed you. What did or didn't they do? How did they approach praise, feedback, and constructive criticism?

Next, think about the colleagues and coworkers you've worked with. How have they responded to their managers, both good and bad? This can give you an insight into some of the common themes in successful management.

Of course, it's also important to recognise that different people will respond to different management styles. Similarly, it's worth bearing in mind concepts of a 'good' or 'successful' manager can be subjective. Someone who is likeable but doesn't get results isn't necessarily a good manager and vice versa.

5 effective ways of managing people

Let's keep in mind this concept of management behaviours and how they can be used to get the best out of a team. Below, we've highlighted five effective ways that you can manage people.

While this is not a comprehensive list, and it may not be applicable in all situations, it is a good starting point for those looking to increase their awareness of management styles. Remember, individuals may not always respond in the same way, and a good manager must be versatile enough to adapt their approach.

1. Lead by example

A good manager will hold themselves to the same standards as the rest of their team. By showing behaviours such as a strong work ethic, good organisational skills, honesty, and openness, you can inspire similar behaviours in those who report to you.

Conversely, you should avoid saying one thing and doing another, or promising to do something and not following through. Strong managers get stuck in, take responsibility, and follow the values of the company.

2. Listen to your team

Leadership doesn't mean simply barking out orders and expecting others to jump to attention. Managing others means listening to what they have to say, whether it's their ideas, concerns, or overall feelings, and taking it on board.

People like to feel heard and that their opinions matter. What's more, part of being in a team is collaborating with others and contributing towards a common goal. A manager who can guide this co-working and ensure everyone feels they have a voice is a valuable asset.

3. Involve your team

Decision-making is an important quality in a management role. However, taking sole control over decisions that impact your team isn't the best approach. Instead, involve your team when you need to take action and get their ideas and opinions.

Not only will this involvement help your team feel engaged and valued, but it will also give you valuable insights into how they're feeling about upcoming decisions. It means you can make a more informed decision and ensure that two-way communication is established.

4. Delegate

Management is often about knowing the strengths and weaknesses of your team and making plans accordingly. It's impossible for you to do everything yourself, and trying to do so means you're leaving valuable resources untapped. Delegation means drawing on the strengths of everyone in your team to deliver the best possible results.

Understanding what can and cannot be delegated, who will excel in particular areas, and how you can deliver and ask for feedback are all vital skills for a manager.

5. Be honest and sincere

Ultimately, to foster strong and trusting working relationships, sincerity and honesty are two essential qualities. It's as important to be honest when things are going well as when they are not; trust is hard to gain and easy to lose.

By treating others with respect, following through on your promises, and owning up to your mistakes, you can show your sincerity. Talk positively about your colleagues, give feedback in a measured and meaningful way, and take responsibility for your team and your actions.

Tips on managing difficult people

When written down in an article such as this, advice on how to manage people seems pretty straightforward. However, in practice, it can often be much harder, particularly if you have someone who is 'difficult' to manage.

If you're finding someone particularly hard to manage, there are a few strategies that you can try. Generally, it's about finding a management style that best suits all involved, as well as recognising the limitations of what you can do.

Here are some quick tips on how to manage difficult people:

Use empathy. Emotional intelligence is a valuable tool here. You can use it to consider how the other person is feeling – why are they being 'difficult'? Are they simply just going through a hard time? Try to understand why their behaviour is challenging and ask yourself how you'd react in their situation.

Find common ground. Finding a shared interest or common belief is a good way of making a connection with someone. It can show that you're on a similar wavelength to the other person, which means you can better understand their feelings and actions.

Stay calm. Reacting to perceived transgressions can further sour a difficult working relationship. Although the person you're managing may make things tough for you, it's important to react appropriately and calmly. Remember, this doesn't mean you have to passively take rudeness, insubordination, or other challenging behaviours.

Keep it professional. You don't have to be friends with the people that you manage. Ultimately, you're all there to do a job. So long as you're professional and civil, no one can ask any more of you.

Be honest. Difficulties can arise when elements such as miscommunication or false assumptions come into play. Sharing your side of the story with a colleague you're having difficulties with can help to smooth things over.

Deal with conflict. Conflict is a natural process that can happen in all relationships. Don't shy away from such occasions, but instead deal with them in a calm and analytical way. Check out our open step on conflict strategies to learn more.

Managers should provide them the attention they need or deserve from their jobs. It's "head down and get on with it" in the world of farming, where the motto goes. Ideas about how to manage people don't necessarily rise to the top of the farm manager's thoughts.

However, no matter how well planned the farm is, if the appropriate tools are missing,

The company's potential will never be achieved if the right personnel are not in place.

Jane Jenkins, Promar's VP of human resources, is confident in the company's workforce. Management isn't necessary for a company's success, but it can add a lot. Maintaining a healthy work-life balance involves more than just increasing financial incentives like raises and other forms of compensation for employees.of work-life balance and social interactions with coworkers organization's members. Despite this, economic compensation, performance-related remuneration is the most an essential component of many performance management systems because it helps to reinforce the message that skill and performance are critical.

It enables people to be rewarded in accordance with their to their own contributions and abilities. That as well as a similar belief that such financial incentives can actually hinder teamwork due to because of their tendency to focus on themselves, some team members may get disengaged due to their perceptions of their own contributions and the resulting disparity in compensation.

Individuals' personal demands are often the focus of management as well as a lot of expectations that can only be partially met filling the need for economic incentives, which necessitate a higher effort ensure that you are happy in your work and that you are respected and appreciated for contributing to the long-term success of an organization.

Their own difficulties in adolescence Thus, the setting is set and deciding on strategies and possibilities for

Managing personnel will be a key responsibility of the individual employees as well as entire teams performance. It is possible to use a variety of HRM tools and can be implemented to help improve performance, frequently requiring managers and their workers to work together,

in an effort to improve individual and organizational performance. Setting goals is an important part of the process annually or on a monthly basis, virtually universally task-by-task basis if necessary. Setting attainable and attainable goals although performance can be improved by setting goals, this is not always the case.

For the best results, use the PLAN-DO-CHECK-ACT methodology.

Use it for regular review and monitoring as well. Many firms, for example, employ the following methods of fostering individual growth.

CHAPTER TWO

Crucial People Management Skills

You will finally be able to complete the assignment effectively.

If you want to move up the corporate ladder and become an effective manager, you'll need a completely different set of abilities than you currently have.

"People management skills" are a separate set of abilities that must be built via experience and practice in order to be completely developed.

People management skills, also known as 'soft skills', are harder to define than technical skills. They include skills such as communication, trust, and patience, to name a few and put simply they are the skills you need to treat, communicate with and lead your people as a manager for maximum results.

A manager with these skills can be the difference between a team that's frustrated, confused and underperforming and a team that's productive, motivated and engaged.

Crucial People Management skills one must possess:

1) Patience

Patience is one of those skills that everyone thinks they have until work gets really tough. It's true that some are born with more patience than others, but that doesn't mean you can't develop your ability to keep a level head in a stressful situation.

When you feel like others are losing their cool — and you might be right there with them — try the following exercise.

Close your eyes.

Take deep breaths in through your nose and out through your mouth.

Slowly count to 10 in your head (one-Mississippi, two-Mississippi works well here).

This simple technique will help you stay patient and calm during the most trying of circumstances.

2) Good Communication

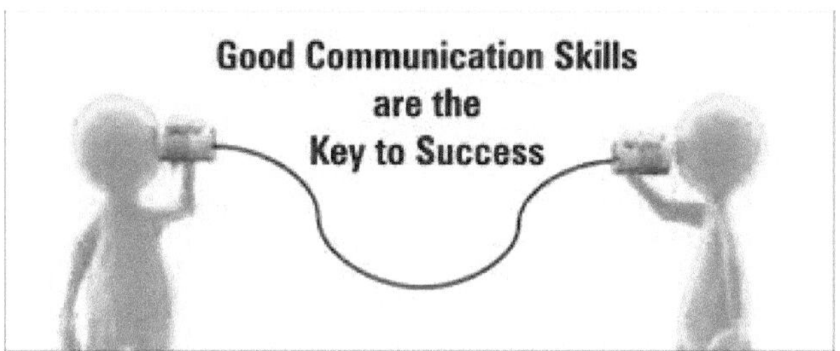

Good communication encompasses a wide range of skills, including:

Your ability to get along with others

Your ability to persuade others

Your ability to get others to listen to your ideas

The clarity of what you say

This last skill is particularly important because time is limited, and the overwhelming presence of mobile devices in our society demands constant communication. Good managers will be as clear as possible in what they say and they will make sure that all employees understand.

3) Ability To Relate

Business is all about people. So being able to relate to other viewpoints is vital to success, whether you're a manager or not. If you struggle at times to relate to another person's attitude, try putting yourself in their shoes. What caused them to feel the way they do? What would make them feel better?

When you can view a situation from a perspective that is not your own — and communicate that you see the value in that perspective — you avoid misunderstandings.

Keep in mind that relating to others doesn't mean you're a pushover. It just means that you can see where the other person is coming from. Don't be afraid to agree to disagree.

4) Flexibility

Flexibility means understanding that there are often multiple ways to complete a task. Just because one team member chooses to tackle a problem differently than you would have doesn't mean that the approach is wrong.

There may be a more efficient way to get the job done, but in most cases, it's the results that really matter.

Flexibility also means being able to adjust quickly to changing circumstances. Don't be so set in your ways that you can't make time to deal with an issue that wasn't on your schedule.

5) Trust

Being a manager is all about trust. You have to trust that your team members have the business's best interest at heart. You have to trust that they will work together to complete any task that comes their way. And finally, you have to trust that all of this will happen without your constant supervision.

Remember, you can't do it all. At some point, you have to delegate. That takes trust — not just in your employees but in yourself and your ability to be an effective leader.

6) Interest In Others

We all want to connect on one level or another, and the best way to do that is by showing interest in others. Here's a simple formula for conveying genuine interest:

- Ask questions
- Consider the answers
- Ask more questions

During the course of your conversations, and for as long as possible thereafter, keep track of pertinent information about your employees so you can ask more questions later. And always remember names, dates, and important events in each person's life.

7) Ability To Listen

As a person in a leadership position, you should always live by the maxim: "We were given two ears, but only one mouth, for a reason." The bulk of your activity, then, should be listening rather than talking.

Take the time to listen to what your employees have to say without interrupting. Then think about what you want to say before responding.

This type of active listen-and-respond is not always easy, but with practice, it can make a difference in how you communicate with your team members and how they communicate with you.

8) Good Judgment

The foundation of good judgment is:

- Looking at the world around you
- Listening to what others have to say
- Learning from that information

Because good judgment is based on sensory signals, it is often described as a "gut feeling." And that's not wrong. Your unconscious mind can process these signals much faster than your conscious mind.

So if you have a "feeling" about something that you can't necessarily explain, use that feeling as a basis for your decision making.

9) Empathy

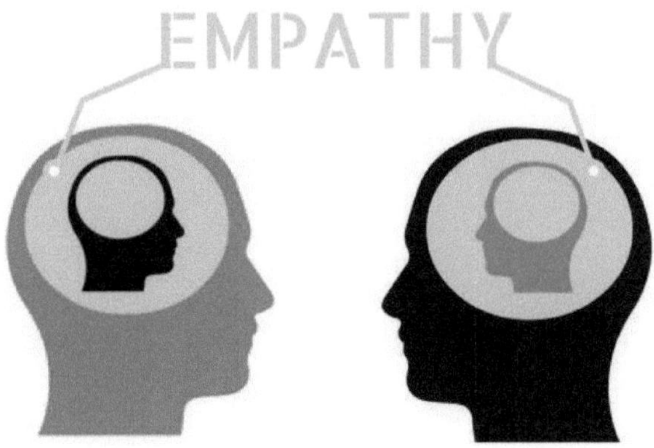

Empathy is defined as the ability to understand and share the feelings of someone else. To put that in simpler terms, think of empathy as compassion. If one of your team members is going through a divorce or their child is seriously ill, it's vital that you show compassion, or empathy, for their situation.

After all, if you were suffering through those issues, you'd want someone to cut you a little slack too. That's what being empathetic is all about: understanding that a team member may be distracted because of challenges outside of work.

Your job as a manager is to make their work life easier for the time being — or help them stay focused — until things settle down.

10) An Open Mind

What does it mean to have an open mind? It's certainly not, "My way or the highway!" An open mind is predicated on the idea that you may not have all the answers, or even the best answer for a given situation. Someone else's notion of what to do may be better than yours.

When you keep an open mind—and make sure that your team members know you have an open mind—it creates trust and respect. Your employees will know that their viewpoint, their feedback, and their suggestions are valued and will be used if at all possible.

When you're known for your open mind, you'll also be known as approachable and easy to work with.

11) Leadership Skills

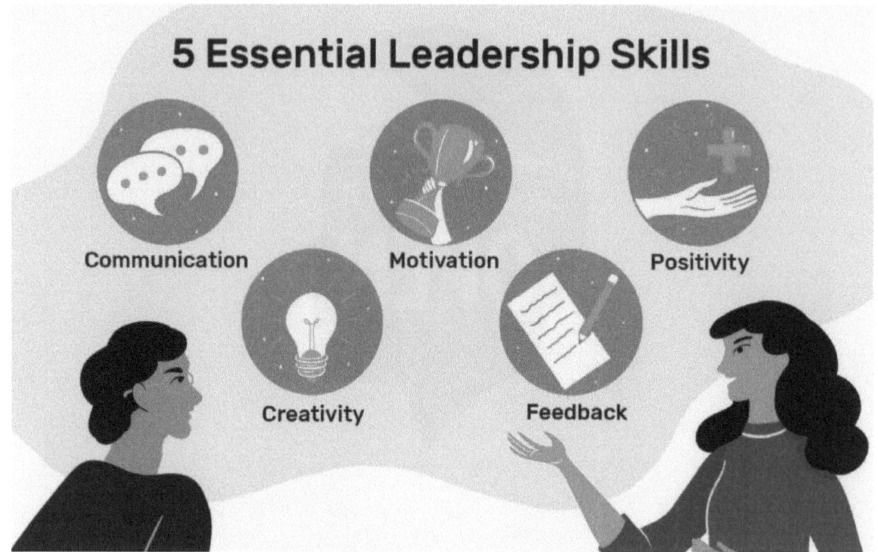

One of the most important people management skills you can develop is the ability to lead effectively. Effective leaders motivate their team to do great things. Ineffective leaders often have undermotivated, underperforming, disengaged teams.

But, like all the skills on this list, you can develop and strengthen your leadership skills. All it takes is an understanding of what motivates your team members, a willingness to make improvements, and plenty of practice.

Here are some simple ways to develop your leadership skills:

- Give employees what they need to succeed
- Be optimistic
- Give praise where praise is due
- Lead by example
- Be decisive
- Be confident in your abilities

Don't feel overwhelmed if you're not doing any of these things right now. Choose one and work on it until it becomes a habit. Then choose another trait from the list and practice it for a few weeks. Take it one step at a time and your leadership skills will improve dramatically.

12) Honesty

Honesty is essential if you want to build a strong team that trusts you and trusts each other. So treat others how you would want to be treated and exhibit honesty in all things.

That means telling the truth in good and bad situations. It also means telling the truth when it's not in your best interest to do so. But when your team sees you being honest at all times, they'll look to your example and follow your behavior.

That will improve the way they work and the way they deal with each other. With honesty — from both you and your employees — your team will draw together and be able to conquer any problem in its path.

13) Problem-Solving Skills

Being a manager means solving problems. It's basically the foundation of your job. You have to figure out how to best schedule your employees, how to set up and manage your inventory, how to track your employees' work hours, how to calculate payroll, and a whole host of other management issues.

Each and every one of these is a problem you must resolve. Without strong problem-solving skills, you'll never get anything done.

So be proactive. If you see a way to improve upon an existing process or you recognize a potential problem before it becomes a real issue, take steps to fix the situation. And if you need to better develop your problem-solving skills, ask a friend, mentor, or higher-up to help you improve.

14) Ability To Adapt

Flexibility and adaptability may seem like the same thing, but they're actually very different. While flexibility means acknowledging the myriad ways to get things done, adaptability means rolling with the changing circumstances.

Within the business itself, an effective leader with strong management skills needs to be able to adapt her leadership style to the personalities on her team. In a larger sense, she must also be able to adapt to new opportunities and new challenges.

Revising your corporate, business, and functional strategies to reflect the changing needs of your customers is a prime example of adaptability in action.

15) Supportiveness

Whether you run a restaurant, a retail chain, or a call center, things will go wrong. A project may fall apart. A customer may get angry. An employee may make an unintentional, though serious, mistake.

It's when your team is at their lowest that your support becomes essential. Reassure them. Encourage them. Bring them together as a team. Be the solid foundation they need to feel secure in their abilities again.

And this doesn't just apply to their work lives. It applies to their personal lives as well. Sometimes, family issues, health problems, or just time and unforeseen occurrences will affect the way your employees work.

The type of support you give for these personal concerns may be different from the support you give for business matters, but the result is the same: inspiration to continue doing their job to the best of their ability.

16) Macro-management

You may be unfamiliar with the word macromanagement, but we're certain you're familiar with its antonym: micromanagement. Micromanagement is a manager's tendency to closely observe and control the work of their employees.

Macro management, on the other hand, is a more independent style of organization. Managers step back and give employees the freedom to do their jobs how they see fit. As long as employees reach the desired result, the manager doesn't have to "hold their hands" or hover over their shoulders looking for mistakes.

This is good for your employees because it gives them the freedom to solve problems, perfect their skills, and become the best team member they can be.

Of course, just like micromanagement, you can take macro management to the extreme if you adopt a laissez-faire attitude in which you always let things take their own course, without ever monitoring situations.

A good manager develops a balanced view and practice of micro-and macro management and understands when to apply both.

17) Accountability

Accountability means taking responsibility for your work and the work of your employees.

As a manager, you serve as a role model for everyone on your team. If you claim accountability when the job is going well but pass the buck when the job is going badly, your employees will notice.

Effective managers take responsibility for failures as well as successes. If the failures begin to outnumber the successes, the manager will take steps to fix the root cause of the problem and inspire their employees to improve.

A lack of accountability at the managerial level erodes the confidence your team has in you — and in the business as a whole. This can create a "me first" attitude in your employees because they will tend to follow the example of those in authority.

You can avoid this issue altogether by being a good role model and always taking responsibility for your actions — and the actions of your team — whether good or bad.

18) Positivity

Positivity in the workplace is crucial if you want your business to succeed. Positivity reflects in everything your team does — from customer-facing activities down to taking out the garbage. And when it's lacking, everyone will feel it.

If you want to encourage positivity in your employees, you need to first exhibit positivity yourself. For example, if you're facing a difficult project or a deadline is rapidly approaching, don't focus on the negative and start to complain.

Instead, get excited about the prospect of finding a new and unique solution or working hard to complete everything before the deadline. Shift your perspective and don't view these challenges as stumbling blocks or obstacles. Instead, see them as opportunities to excel.

When you exercise positivity come what may, the attitude will rub off on your employees and motivate them to greatness.

19) Approachability

As a manager, you are the leader of your team. That means that, at some point, one of your employees is going to come to you with problems and questions. You're going to need to give guidance and direction.

But how will you receive them? Will you be brusque and dismissive? Or will you be welcoming and approachable?

Being open and approachable — even when you're already busy — is the quality that builds goodwill, positivity, and loyalty in your team.

Regardless of what you're doing, try to give your full attention to anyone who comes to you with a question or problem. If you have a hard time doing this, put yourself in their shoes.

Imagine how you would feel going to your supervisor (or your supervisor's supervisor) with a dilemma in the company. You'd likely feel nervous and apprehensive. In that state of mind, how would you want your superior to act — dismissive about the issue or approachable and willing to talk?

If you simply can't be interrupted at the moment, apologize and reassure your team member that you want to hear what they have to say. Then, make an appointment to talk and be sure to keep it.

20) Organization

The word "organize" has many definitions, but for the purpose of business, it means coordinating the activities of a group of people efficiently. Some people are just naturally organized. Others are not.

Regardless of which end of that spectrum you occupy, you can improve your organizational skills with the help of the Sling app.

Sling is a scheduling and time clock app designed with busy managers in mind. But Sling is about more than just making sure every slot in your rotating shift schedule is filled. It's about simplifying every aspect of the scheduling, distribution, time-tracking, and communication processes.

Sling's core features include:

- Shifts
- Time Clock
- Messages
- Newsfeed
- Tasks

The Sling app incorporates all these features into an intuitive scheduling tool that helps you create clear, easy-to-read schedules that can be quickly posted to the cloud for convenient storage and distribution. You can even control who can view the schedule and who can make changes.

Sling also provides a central location where your team members can indicate when they're available to work. The Sling app then uses that information to remind you about double-bookings, unavailability, and time-off requests when you sit down to create the schedule.

But Sling's benefits don't end there. The Sling Time Clock feature makes it easier than ever for team members to clock in and clock out. They can even use their own mobile device!

CHAPTER THREE

MANAGING TEAMS

Defining a team as a group of people who have a common goal is a good place to start when learning how to manage people, who share a shared goal and who must collaborate in order to achieve your goals

While managers' empowerment of teams or individuals might result in improved performance, this is not always the case.

A manager's or team leader's job is to:

- create cohesive teams
- focus on increasing productivity and results
- increasing the use of both individual and group efforts
- Rather than focusing on faults, focus on your strengths.

Numerous investigations into the dynamics of teams have been conducted and the roles each member of the team plays; the most important Dr. Meredith Belbin's work is the most well-known of these 2004, and his subsequent publications were managed by the same studies. The purpose of this chapter is not to describe the team an individual member's point of view but still functioning as part of a team

Focus on how to manage teams. Regarding this, It is premised that Belbin's roles provide useful insight into how individuals working in teams function and their natural qualities.

However, it is evident that full empowerment must be promoted from the top of the organization in order to become part of the corporate culture and business philosophy of the company. This includes awards, goal setting, appraisals, and so on. In spite of the fact that many firms are keen on entrusting their staff with greater responsibility, this can lead to a loss of control and erosion of authority for their managers, despite the fact that they recognize the positive aspects of empowerment.

For example, sports teams or an orchestral concert offer extreme examples of how teams and teamwork may routinely accomplish far more than the sum of the individual members in getting a job done. As a result, teams may be formed for a specific project and then disbanded after the project is finished, allowing the team members to join new groups. Project work is a fantastic illustration of this cycle of team formation and dissolution. The team works together to achieve a specific goal and then disbands after the project is complete. The six stages of such team dynamics are depicted in Tuckman and Jensen's original 1977 publication, as well as subsequent research. The members of each stage are depicted in their typical mannerisms.

During the "forming" stage, the group's members are anxious about who fits where, who is joining the group, and the relative position of each member. This stage reflects the underdevelopment of teamwork. First-stage symptoms include extremely polite, embarrassed, and passionate members of the team who have made little progress thus far. Consensus and reliance on the team leader are also a part of the process.

Even in high-performing teams and even if the members have worked together before, this "storming" stage is a natural occurrence. Roles are frequently questioned and members put one another to the test. Before greater performance can be achieved it is often necessary to address team issues that have arisen as a result of a lack of attention to these issues. Participants begin to experiment with new ways of working and accomplishing tasks as the conflict progresses into stage two, which is marked by conflict, active debate and discussion, rebellion against the leader and polarized opinions.

It is now that the team has worked out any concerns, and the areas of dispute have been stitched up. The group has a lot of support from each other, and the attention now shifts to the task at hand and how individuals may help one other.

This phase is known as "norming" because it involves the establishment of standard operating procedures and workflows. Shared responsibilities for leadership, an openness to new ideas and methods of problem solving are some of the telltale indications of the third stage.

Teamwork has matured and the completely productive group is now referred to as "performing" once the previous stages have gone. They are more concerned with attaining their goals, and cooperation among the members of the team is second nature because everyone knows each other's talents and weaknesses. The group's roles are functional and ad hoc. Clearly, this is the position that team leaders seek to achieve as quickly as possible. One sign that the team has reached this level of development is the presence of a calm and focused culture, as well as the accomplishments being talked about most frequently.

In the original work, there was no stage 5, but it was later identified as something to avoid when it comes to "dorming" or falling asleep. It emphasizes the necessity of including people in the decision-making process concerning their actions and methods. When a team is nearing the end of its life, members may want to extend the group's existence by putting in more effort to keep the group going.

Mourning happens when a team's performance is disrupted by members departing to take on new work, members being unclear about their future roles, and usually by the overall break-up of the team, the shared experience, and ending of working friendships. This final stage is called "mourning" Despite this, the team's overall performance suffers if the group gradually disintegrates.

It's possible that you'll be working on finishing up loose ends, celebrating accomplishments, experiencing sadness, or making plans for new teams during this phase. The final step of team formation is often overlooked because the major work or project has been accomplished, and so the team's central focus has diminished.

Managing a team's performance and knowing where it stands in reference to these six stages are essential if you want to maximize its output and provide everyone the freedom they need to carry out their responsibilities to the best of their abilities.

A team approach is a strong and decisive management style.

• Stress is decreased as difficulties are shared.

• More ideas are developed, therefore the potential to innovate is increased.

A team approach is a strong and decisive management style.

There are several advantages to working as a team to address complex or multi-disciplinary issues, such as resolving interpersonal difficulties, clarifying responsibilities, and improving personal contributions.

Building an effective team takes time and effort, since it necessitates careful planning, the development of strong working relationships, and the establishment of an environment conducive to productive teamwork.

A team's "operational health" can be assessed by using the short checklist provided below, which asks whether or not the group:

– this week, this month, this year? •

• Can you tell me what to do?

• Do you feel in command of its future course?

• Is there a two-way exchange?

Possibilities for alternative suggestions?

Use your feelings wisely?

In the workplace, how often do you compliment your coworkers for doing a good job?

• Are you avoiding the expression of negative emotions?

• How would you feel if you were constantly afraid and depressed? Are your expectations crystal-clear?

• Do you agree that its standards are reasonable?

Is the hierarchy well-structured and the work distributed evenly throughout the organization?

Individual strengths and flaws can be discussed openly without fear of retribution?

• Do we know one another better than the average person?

• How well did you organize your time?

When it comes to resources, how do you maximize them?

• Do you know who you are?
Complaining and moaning excessively?
• Do you have a strategy for resolving conflicts?
Place a high value on outcomes?
• Have fun and cooperate?
If a project is long-term and strategic, a more in-depth look into the teamwork and how the organization supports it may be required.

Culture

- Do employees have a sense of belonging to the company and its success?
- a direct benefit to the organization or themselves?
- How many people in your organization believe they share a shared goal?
- with their coworkers and the collective?
- Are you a part of a cohesive group?
- Is work assigned according to the level of skill of each individual instead of one's position inside the company?
- Are your employees free to express themselves in relation to the business?
- Innovation and entrepreneurship are encouraged by the organization.
- a culture of innovation in the workplace?
- Is there a sense of personal accountability among employees at work?
- Quality is focused in every area of the product organization?

Organization

- Is your organization's structure conducive to fostering innovation?
- how well are you performing?
- Is the structure of the organization flexible enough to deal with altering expectations?

There may be a problem with the structure.

• Do employees understand their responsibilities?
Can you identify areas in which your organization's structure exacerbates rather than alleviates problems?
do they exist?
How effective are the procedures and management practices?

What is the goal of completing a task?

• Are you always looking for new ways to improve your organization?

People

• Is the workforce well-trained and knowledgeable?

do the best job possible at what they're supposed to be doing

• Is it clear to employees what their roles are and how they fit into the wider picture of the company's performance?

• Is there a customer service orientation among your employees?

Is it possible to identify persons who have the potential to succeed?

In what ways are the employees motivated to perform at their best?

expressing gratitude, providing constructive criticism, and so on?

In general, are employees aware of what they are expected to do in the workplace?

What are the accepted norms?

Systems: Systems (recruitment, promotion, planning, management information, and control) in your business are up to date and effective.

motivate your employees to do their best work?

• Is there uniformity in these systems across the company?

Is there a clear payoff for good work?

Where are you working?

• How often does the company do system reviews?

and see to it that they both support one another?

As a team leader, you must keep track of all of your team's tasks as well as the progress of those tasks.

Tips on how to manage a team successfully

And now, for some team management techniques for you to try.

1) Assemble the right team

The most effective way to ensure that the tasks you set out will be delivered at top quality is to have the right people doing them. A crucial step, selecting the most suitable group of people will avoid any skill gaps within your team.

2) Trust your team to do their job

Delegating tasks is at the top of the team management skills list—so remember to do it. Avoid micromanaging as it can be rather intrusive, and demonstrates a lack of trust in your team's abilities. However, offer support as some people require more instructions than others. You have to find the perfect balance.

3) Be consistent, but use different approaches

Take into consideration the different types of personalities that make up your team, and apply the diversity to your managing style. For example, there will be people who don't take constructive criticism as well as others, so tailor your approach when providing feedback. In saying this however, you do have to be consistent in your team management techniques. The same behaviors need to be rewarded and/or discouraged throughout your team for your management to be effective.

4) Recognize achievements

If someone's doing a good job, acknowledge it. Recognizing efforts illustrates to your team that you are paying attention to them, and that you appreciate their hard work. It can be as little as announcing it in front of their peers, to something more special, like certificates or vouchers. Just remember to be consistent with this, because the last thing you want is for someone thinking that you're playing favorites.

5) Focus your team on a unified goal

On top of their own individual targets, ensure there is at least one goal for your team to work on together. This type of unity will enhance communication and collaboration within your group, and remind them that they are part of a team.

Work together towards the same goal!

6) Improve rapport

I'm not saying you have to be best mates with your staff, but getting to know them on a personal level can help strengthen teamwork. Allocate time outside of work for some team bonding sessions. These types of activities can make your team feel comfortable with each other, and with you. If people don't comfortable, your team won't be sustainable.

7) Create an open dialogue

Clear communication is vital for obvious reasons—everyone needs to know what's going on. Regular updates can help prevent any issues that may arise, and forecast the outcome of your work. Also, be open to feedback from your team members. A two-way relationship can help solidify trust, and also improve your team management techniques.

8) Foster development

Not only is managing talent a crucial factor for the business's overall growth, but it can also ensure that your team members are happy in their roles.

Offering support and training shows that you prize their talent, and want them to continue working for you. Up-skilling and growing expertise can only really be beneficial.

9) Use a team-based productivity software

This may already be a given in most businesses, but using a team-based productivity software (like Zenkit!) is a handy way to centralize resources, and keep everyone updated with work progress. Depending on what type of team you are managing—whether the work is project-based or it's simple day-to-day business operations—you will find the benefits of using a project management tool or a workflow management system rewarding. These solutions equip you, and your team, with the tools needed to organize, schedule, and execute projects and business activity.

10) Set an example

The best way to communicate your expectations to your team is to show them. As the manager, your behavior will have a great effect on how your team conduct their work, and interact with each other. For instance, you can't expect your staff to take punctuality seriously if you keep showing up to meetings late. Not only will they think that tardiness is acceptable, but they may start to question your integrity as a manager. Their only way to know what you deem the ideal worker is if you influence it through your actions.

CHAPTER FOUR

Conflict

Conflict is a situation in which two or more parties or organizations' interests are at odds with one another. Hostility, bad attitudes, disagreement, violence, competition, and misunderstanding are all examples of this expression.

When referring to an industrial conflict, we are referring to any kind of disagreement between employers and their workers or between employees themselves. Employees of multinational corporations (MNCs) come from a wide range of countries and backgrounds. This means that differences in values, beliefs, and working habits might lead to conflict.

A lack of openness and trust between people, as well as the managers' failure to respond to their employees' needs and expectations have all been blamed for the destructive and dysfunctional effects of conflict. Non-cooperation between groups can lead to a decrease in productivity. Conflicts can also lead to a decrease in productivity and a distraction from the task at hand. Conflicts should therefore be avoided in accordance with the customary attitude. Tasks, rules, laws, processes, and authority relationships that are properly structured can help identify and resolve conflicts.

In today's society, conflict is viewed as a good element in the workplace. Conflicts, according to this perspective, are essential to a group's ability to function efficiently. Conflict is fostered by this strategy. In order for the group to be functional, self-critical, and creative, there must be a minimum acceptable amount of disagreement among its members. Functional conflict is the name given to this sort of dispute. On the other hand, disagreements that have a negative impact on the group's ability to perform are considered dysfunctional.

Conflict Types or Levels

Managers in multinational corporations (MNCs) spend 20-30% of their time resolving conflicts.

As a result, it is critical for managers to be aware of the many types of conflict they face in order to develop effective strategies for dealing with them. Conflicts can fall into one of several categories, as listed below:

a. Conflict at the individual level

a. Conflict between individuals

c. Conflict at a group level.

d. Dispute at the organizational level

1. Conflict at the level of the individual: every individual is riven by internal conflict. Conflicts can arise when an individual is unable to make decisions due to a lack of motivation or a lack of drive. Uncertainty about duties and objectives, an inability to analyze the numerous options available, and an unwillingness to accept the decisions of the firm can all contribute to these disputes.

There are three main types of conflict that can occur between coworkers:

Frustration occurs when an employee is unable to carry out his or her own desires. This is the most extreme form of unhappiness, and as a result, it can lead to conflict inside the person. When an individual's motivations or drives are stymied, frustration ensues. They can be physical or mental/social-psychological in nature. Expatriates working for multinational corporations may become irritated if they aren't able to operate to the same standards as their parent company.

These constraints may be imposed by the host country or organization owing to cultural, societal, or physical factors.

Conflicting goals might arise when an employee has to work for more than one objective. Employees may be unable to make decisions on how to accomplish a goal as a result of this form of conflict, which has both positive and negative aspects. Employees may become perplexed as to whether they are being sent on a foreign assignment or being promoted within the parent organization. Or if an employee gets promoted but must relocate to a foreign subsidiary, he or she may feel conflicted between the positive aspects of the promotion and the negative aspects of having to leave his or her home and family.

One individual in an organization is required to perform his or her job with a specific set of values and behaviors, and these values and behaviors can conflict with each other. There is no way to meet one expectation without rejecting the other in the case of a conflict between the expectations of the role and the expectations of the individual. Role conflict occurs when the requirements of the role are understood, yet they cannot be complied with for one or the other cause.

In the event of a foreign subsidiary, an international assignee is expected to match the criteria of the parent firm as well. The roles and the criteria for their execution are established in the parent nation; however, when they are carried out in the host country, cultural, social, and other variables unique to the host country may cause conflict. Role conflict is more likely to develop when the foreign assignee is familiar with the customs and environment of the host country and also realizes that using parent country methods may not work successfully in the host country.

Two or more people are involved in an interpersonal dispute, which is the most prevalent sort of conflict. The corporation may set up scenarios where two people find themselves in conflict. ' Interpersonal conflicts can arise between the local manager and the parent country manager in multinational corporations (MNCs) because of disagreements over goals and objectives, varying performance standards, a lack of effective communication and information sharing, and various cultural differences, to name a few. It is not uncommon for communications between parent companies and their Japanese foreign subsidiaries to take place entirely in Japanese, with no translation provided. When it comes to communication and decision-making, host country managers are even more restricted than their counterparts in the host country itself.

Disputes develop as a result of this, and the consequences can be severe, such as employee dissatisfaction or even resignation.

There are three types of conflicts that can occur in a group: conflict between two or more people, conflict between two or more people working toward a common objective, and conflict between two or more people working toward the same goal. A group's members' behavior is influenced by the group's members, other groups, and even the entire organization. There are two sorts of conflicts that take place at the group level:
In both cases, there are internal and external conflicts.

Conflicts within an organization can occur amongst its members. It's like interpersonal disagreement, but the parties involved are all members of the same social group. The root causes of intrapersonal conflict are the same as those that lead to conflict with others.

Conflicts within an organization's many divisions are referred to as "inter group conflicts. Conflicts can occur between different levels of an organization, such as between middle managers and upper or lower-level managers, or they can occur between distinct functional areas, such as between the marketing department and the manufacturing department. Intergroup disputes may arise due to a variety of factors, including access to and share in resources, favorable time schedules, and differences in values, beliefs, and cultures.

Conflicts at the organizational level:

This type of conflict happens between organizations that are in some way dependent on each other. An increasing number of disagreements arise when a parent company's international subsidiaries compete with each other. Disagreements may also emerge between various international branches of a multinational corporation (MNC).

A lack of information facilities, a monopoly of the parent firm, and other environmental issues such as various norms and regulations may lead to conflicts between the headquarters of a corporation and its subsidiaries. Trade unions, government agencies in the host country, or any other organizations that have an impact on the corporation may also get in the way of the parent company or subsidiary. MNCs and local governments might have disagreements over policy, laws, and regulations.

Conflicts in multinational corporations are caused by the following factors:

Conflict can be sparked by a breakdown in communication. Disagreements may emerge between citizens of the parent country and those of the host country as a result of inadequate communication. A lack of information about the local environment may also be an issue for HCNs. As with PCNs, it may lead to interpersonal disputes if they are unable to convey the necessary procedures or expectations of the parent firm. Conflicts may arise as a result of differences in the semantics of the languages spoken in the two countries.

Expatriate role conflict can also be caused by a mismatch between expectations and actual behavior in the host country. Conflicts between local managers and expatriates might also arise. The parent company's desire to exert control over the subsidiary can also lead to conflict. People from different countries have distinct values, social norms, cultures and behaviors, which can lead to conflict.

Conflicts might arise when PCNs have a skewed relationship with local personnel.

There is a structural component to conflict:

a. Conflict is more likely to occur in large organizations.

Conflicts in the workplace can be exacerbated by increasing decentralization of decision making and employee autonomy.

As a result, it might lead to conflict if duties aren't clearly established. Each employee, regardless of country, should have their duties, responsibilities, and accountability clearly defined and assigned to them.

Competition for finite resources, such as funds and facilities, leads to conflict and divisions among those who share them and must compete for them, as shown in example d above.

For PCNs and HCNs, there will be industrial conflicts if there are differences in policies on human resources.

Management of conflict

There are two ways to deal with disagreements in the workplace or in an organization.

The first step is to take a. preventative measures b. Curative measures

Preventive measures by MNC are aimed at preventing conflicts from becoming dysfunctional. The sooner conflicts are settled, the less likely they are to result in damage. The following is a breakdown of the two measures:

Anti-Conflict Preventive Actions: the following measures can be adopted by the organization to avoid conflicts:

Conflicting parties can work together to achieve similar aims.
It's possible for management to discover common goals for the groups to agree on and re-establish effective communication.

Reduction of interdependence: interdependence is a major cause of inter-group conflict. The less interdependence there is, the less likely there is to be a conflict. To ensure that subsidiaries may make decisions that are in the best interests of the parent firm, multinational corporations should provide them enough autonomy to consider the local context of the host country when formulating policies and making decisions. Because of the differences in culture and climate, the policies of one country cannot be applied to another.

Foreign workers should receive cross-cultural training to help them better comprehend the realities in their new place of residence. It is possible to give this training before or after arriving in the host country. This would assist expatriates better grasp their host country's environment and, as a result, minimize their disputes with HCNs by helping them frame and adopt decisions in line with host country conditions.

All personnel, including expatriates, should have their roles well defined. As a rule, all employees should be made aware of their specific duties, responsibilities, and authority. Interpersonal and collective conflict will be reduced as a result.

Members of an organization will have more open and free communication if they trust each other. If there are any misconceptions, everyone and every group should be encouraged to openly interact with each other. It helps them to grasp one other's concerns in a more comprehensive way. MNCs are responsible for ensuring an open line of communication between their home country and the country where they are doing business. All messages should be sent in a language that is understood by locals, or the company should arrange for translation.

It is imperative that multinational corporations (MNCs) treat all employees equally, regardless of whether they are HCNs or PCNs. Conflicts will be less likely as a result of this. PCNs, on the other hand, are always employed in senior positions in foreign companies by countries that adhere to an ethnocentric approach. It may cause HCNs to harbor feelings of resentment.

Conflicts between groups might arise from the sharing of scarce resources. The company should aim to grow resources, or make the best use of limited resources between several groups.

A multinational corporation (MNC) should make an attempt to coordinate the activities of its many divisions. Coordinating operations inside a unit is critical to its success.

Groups can be restructured by placing members who share a same interest in one group. In this method they will have common interest and aim, thereby reducing conflicts.

Corporate citizenship fosters a sense of camaraderie among employees, which reduces the likelihood of workplace disputes.

Collective bargaining is a method used by employers and employee representatives to try and come to an agreement and aids in the resolution of issues and prevention of industrial conflicts and disputes.

b. Therapeutic measures or methods of resolving disputes:

After a conflict occurs, corrective procedures are implemented. There are several names for this process, including dispute resolution.

Managers must be familiar with a variety of conflict resolution techniques and know when to employ each in different circumstances. Here are some methods for resolving disputes:

One of the most common conflict resolution tactics is to suppress and avoid open conflict. There are differing levels of conflict avoidance in different national cultures.

The Japanese, for example, are less inclined to engage in warfare than the American population. " An avoiding conduct indicates a lack of attention to key concerns and an unwillingness to take action when necessary. In the following instances, avoidance behavior should be adopted:

- It's easier to deal with tension later, when the avoider wishes for the other person to relax.
- However, there are times when further information is needed to make an informed conclusion.
- The disagreement can be resolved more efficiently if it is handled by a third party.

Assertiveness and a lack of cooperation characterize the competitive style. It is a "WIN-LOSE" technique that views conflict in terms of power. It has the potential to be both positive and destructive. Competitiveness, on the one hand, aids in making quick judgments, but it also has the potential to lead to conflict. Powers given to PCNs by the parent business may provide them an advantage over HCNs in the case of a multinational corporation.

In the instance of collaboration, both parties work together to find a solution to the issue that is mutually acceptable. High levels of cooperation and assertiveness characterize this communication style.

Assertiveness is low, while cooperation is high, in this approach. With an accommodating conflict management strategy, managers will have little regard for their own interests. When harmony is a priority, this style is used.

When conflicting parties agree to compromise the situation, they agree to share resources or resolve the disagreement in a way that provides both parties a degree of victory and defeat. When both collaboration and competition fail to succeed in resolving issues, this strategy is often pursued. Parties also agree to a short-term solution to the problem until a more permanent answer is found.

Government of host country can appoint an inquiry board or court to look into conflict. 6. Either the government or one or both sides to the conflict can compel an investigation be carried out.

In mediation, a third party intervenes to help the parties resolve their differences. The primary responsibility of a mediator is to facilitate a voluntary settlement of a conflict.

Conciliation and arbitration are used to combine two conflicting groups in the industry so that there is no interruption in production, distrust, or other negative consequences. Employers and employee representatives meet with the help of a third party to try and reach an agreement through conciliation. A third-party aided extension of collective bargaining.

There are a number of options for resolving disputes between two parties who are unable to come to an agreement on their own, such as mediation or arbitration, which both parties must accept.

Compelled arbitration or adjudication is utilized when there are weak trade unions. Arbitration that is mandated by law is utilized when all other avenues of dispute resolution have failed to produce a resolution.

Depending on the country, multinational corporations have a varied approach to resolving disputes. A study comparing the styles of Taiwan and the United States indicated that Taiwanese people are more likely to utilize avoiding and compromise styles than Americans. According to the situation, parties involved in the conflict, and the available organizational resources, multinational corporations can take a variety of responses.

The following is a summary of the points made in

When referring to an industrial conflict, we are referring to any kind of disagreement between employers and their workers or between employees themselves. Employees of multinational corporations (MNCs) come from a wide range of countries and backgrounds. This means that differences in values, beliefs, and working habits might lead to conflict.

Conflicts can be classified into four categories: interpersonal, group, and organizational. There are a number of variables that contribute to disputes in multinational corporations: communication gaps, cultural, social, and other environmental differences, lack of resources, lack of cooperation from the parent business, the desire to assume control of the subsidiary, etc. Establishing a single purpose, reducing dependencies, cross cultural training of expatriates, clearly defined roles and trust and communication are just some of the preventative actions that MNCs may do to avoid conflict in the first place.

These strategies include avoiding conflict, competing with each other, cooperating with each other and compromising with each other as well as investigating, meditating, resolving, and arbitration.

AVIOD
CONFLICTS!

CHAPTER FIVE

MANAGING TEAM CONFLICT

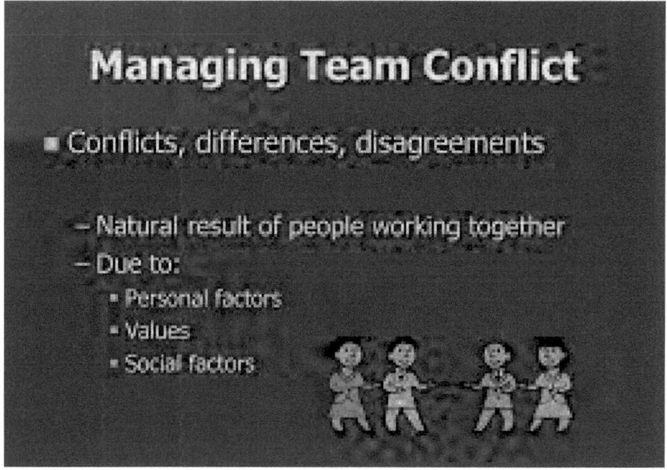

The diversity of resources, knowledge, and ideas that come from working in a team can be a huge advantage, but it can also be a source of friction.

Conflict can emerge for a variety of reasons, and while each team is unique, there are certain general patterns for dealing with conflict, such as:

Poor communication, such as a lack of willingness to provide information, changes in interpretation, information flow, and so on.

Structural elements such as objectives and issues of priority, the involvement levels, reward methods and team size are all factors to consider.

And how they're connected at many levels.

A person's sense of self-worth, for example, their own unique set of aspirations, values, and requirements.

According to some, most managers are aware of their employees' work.

They should take the initiative in resolving their differences. It is important to keep in mind that team conflict does not always be both damaging and inspiring at the same time and ways in which new organizational processes and development can be adopted. But this will not become a reality in the future.

When left unchecked, the situation can quickly spiral out of control.

To feel defeated and distrust grows, which creates a hostile atmosphere.

Even a well-established and well-functioning team can be suddenly demolished. It is possible that conflicts will emerge in the following areas:

A lack of understanding or usage of administrative procedures by the team members causes them to be unable to carry out their responsibilities.

• A team with insufficient resources to accomplish the task, take on the task at hand. For a brief while, this may work, Over the course of time, this could be considered acceptable.

One of the most important things to keep in mind while dealing with team disagreement is that the true issue isn't the conflict itself, but rather how it is handled. Failure to manage conflict effectively results in a loss of team energy, deterioration of good relationships, and the inability to complete the work. Unresolved disagreement, perceived betrayal of trust, and other such issues can lead to conflict within a team.

There are a variety of factors that contribute to interpersonal conflict, such as misunderstanding, personality clashes, divergent moral ideals, chronic stress, and issues with one's own ego. Improved communication skills, team counseling, ceding, adapting, collaborating, listening, responding, and comprehending are some of the cures for resolving problems. Team conflict can be avoided or resolved by following some key guidelines, such as: achieving consensus through collaboration, controlling emotional outbursts, increasing self-esteem, protecting dignity, listening attentively and empathically to concerns and concerns of others, being honest about concerns and removing personal ego from management style, for example. In order to settle conflicts, it's helpful to have a conflict resolution mechanism in place, train team members on human dynamics of working together, and build relationships with challenging team members.

Unresolved disagreement can stifle a team's growth if it goes unaddressed throughout the process.

Small groups of people with complementary abilities who are committed to a single purpose, goals, and approach are known as teams. (1993), according to Katzenbach and Smith

In order to achieve the team's objectives, the members of the team must have a complimentary set of skills. To that end, the group's members must have some say in how they collaborate to achieve their objectives (Syer 1997). To put it another way, teams generate synergy, meaning that the combined efforts of all team members are significantly larger than the sum of their individual efforts (French et al. 2007).

It's important for teams to learn how to disagree without ruining the team's work environment. Researchers have found that high-performing teams are able to mediate their own conflicts while enhancing productivity and enhancing the quality of their interpersonal connections (McDaniel et al.1998). The great majority of employees operate in small groups where their efforts must fit together like the pieces of a picture puzzle. Teams are formed when their work is interconnected and they aim to cultivate a cooperative state known as teamwork. In 1995, (John and Keith).

When a team works well together, it's because each member is able to think and act for the good of the group rather than his or her own self-interest (Singh, 2004).

Change can only occur when there is conflict (McDaniel et al.1998). When handled effectively, disagreement can lead to new ideas for improving organizational procedures, the resolution of ongoing problems, and the opportunity for workers to enhance their abilities (Bowditch & Buono, 1997). Failure to manage conflict effectively results in a loss of team energy, deterioration of good relationships, and the inability to complete the work.

Teams must understand that the focus is not on conflict itself, but rather on conflict management when dealing with team disagreement. It is not the goal of conflict management to reduce conflict, but rather to manage conflict constructively (Rayeski & Bryant, 1994). Resentment between team members can build up if a team leader doesn't handle dispute; this can have a negative impact on the overall effectiveness of the team (Wisinski,

1995).

Conflicts within the Workplace

The word "conflict" elicits a wide range of emotions, including anger, irritation, grief, and pain in many people. If left unresolved, even a minor difference of opinion among coworkers can quickly turn into hostility, inability to cooperate, verbal assaults, and resentment.

In the worst circumstances, it can lead to antagonism and eventually the breakup of the company. Because of this, it is imperative that the conflict be handled quickly. (Problem Solving Team).

Antagonism, discord, clash, and collision are all synonyms for conflict, which refers to a battle, a struggle, or a confrontation between two or more opposed forces. Personality, beliefs, philosophies and religion are only some of the many factors that contribute to conflict. It might also be caused by misinterpretations. A substantial increase in the amount of human contacts where one's perspective is heard has occurred as we have broadened collaborative concepts in our workplaces.

There may be disagreements among newly formed teams as their conversations take them into unfamiliar territory (Peter B. Grazier).

Conflict's Origin

When institutional and retail sales teams work together in the same firm sales offices, they share the same go down or C & F agent, billing system, commercial team, delivery team, and accounting department. They also share a billing system. Both teams seek to provide preference to their own clients or members of their distribution channel. Billing personnel and delivery personnel are subjected to expert pressure in the hope of expediting the completion of orders, even if it means incurring more costs for tiny deliveries or several consignments for deliveries within a single geographical region.

In order to cut operating expenses, the commercial team works to maximize the utilization of space in any carrier and group supplies in one direction. Sales teams are prone to conflict when this happens since some orders are left unfulfilled. At the end of the month, when all the sales team members extract orders from each channel partner or customer in order to meet their monthly goals, this problem is magnified.

Each one of them wants to ensure that the orders he has procured are billed and delivered before the sales are closed by the commercial department at any point. Even if there is only one sort of sales team, this scenario is more apparent when both teams are involved. This is most likely owing to the fact that there are two team leaders, each of whom conveys a sense of our and their own sales (Zameer 2005).

Some of the best ideas come from friction in the workplace. However, instances might develop where conflict in teams becomes interpersonally damaging and leads to diminished effectiveness. This is especially true when team members start assaulting one another or making disparaging remarks about one another's talents, abilities, or overall performance. Individuals and the team as a whole will be negatively affected by this behavior. Conflicts in the workplace are generally created by a person's professional role or organizational structure, rather than their personality.

Problems in the workplace are often blamed on the individual, but this isn't always the case.

Interpersonal conflict in teams can be caused by a lack of structure, lack of resources, poor organizational environment, or an improper organizational strategy. This is a common cause of interpersonal conflict in teams." Due to unique working styles, some of the differences between team members may result in animosity or friction amongst them. There are times when disagreements between members of a team can't be blamed only on their roles, responsibilities, or personalities. There will be annoyances and challenges along the way (West 1996).

CHAPTER SIX

Causes of Team Conflict

Causes of Team Conflict?

S. No	Causes of conflict	S. No	Causes of Conflict
1	Poor or no communication	8	Lack of leadership and management
2	Lack of problem solving skills	9	**Boredom**
3	Lack of clarity in purpose, goals, objectives,	10	Team members not challenged, not interested
4	Lack of team and individual roles	11	Lack of skills and abilities in team members
5	**Lack of resources** and sources for help and support	12	**Personality**
6	Poor or lack of time management	13	**Personal problems**
7	Turnover	14	**Differing objectives**, Etc.

Some of these can be seen as both cause and result of conflict.

Conflicts in the Workplace

Poor communication, a desire for power, unhappiness with management style, weak leadership, a lack of transparency, and a shift in leadership are all causes of conflict in the workplace (N.S.B.A. 2007).

Conflict is a common occurrence on teams. Conflict itself can be defined as antagonistic interactions in which one party tries to block the actions or decisions of another party. Bringing conflicts out into the open where they can be resolved is an important part of the team leader's or manager's job.

There are two basic types of team conflict: substantive (sometimes called task) and emotional (or relationship).

Substantive conflicts arise over things such as goals, tasks, and the allocation of resources. When deciding how to track a project, for example, a software engineer may want to use a certain software program for its user interface and customization capabilities. The project manager may want to use a different program because it produces more detailed reports. Conflict will arise if neither party is willing to give way or compromise on his position.

Emotional conflicts arise from things such as jealousy, insecurity, annoyance, envy, or personality conflicts. It is emotional conflict when two people always seem to find themselves holding opposing viewpoints and have a hard time hiding their personal animosity. Different working styles are also a common cause of emotional conflicts. Julia needs peace and quiet to concentrate, but her office mate swears that playing music stimulates his creativity. Both end up being frustrated if they can't reach a workable resolution.

Conflict Can Be Beneficial

Not all conflict is negative. Just as some forms of stress can be beneficial, so can some types of conflict. Eustress is a positive reaction to stress that generates a desire to achieve and overcome challenges. For instance, some people find that they produce their best work when a deadline is looming and the pressure to produce gets the adrenaline flowing. Team conflicts can also produce positive results when the conflict centers on substantive issues. Conflict can spark new ideas and generate creativity.

On the other hand, when people feel they cannot disagree or offer different opinions, new ideas cannot emerge. Groupthink is the mindset that develops when people put too much value on team consensus and harmony. It is common when individuals are afraid to go against what most group members—especially dominant members—think. Some degree of conflict helps teams avoid groupthink and forces the group to make choices based on rational decision making.

If there is too much cooperation, the best ideas may never get shared and team effectiveness is sacrificed for the sake of efficiency. For the same reasons that diversity bestows benefits on a workforce, a mix of ideas and opinions improves team performance and decision making. If there is too much conflict, however, then nothing can get done. Employees on the team become less satisfied and motivated and may turn to social loafing or may even work against other members out of sheer frustration.

Common Causes of Conflict

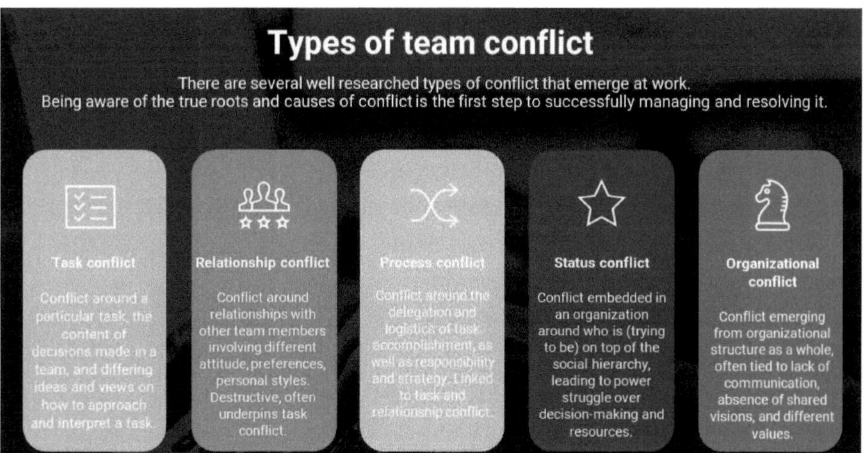

Some common causes of negative conflict in teams are identified as follows:

Conflict often arises when team members focus on personal (emotional) issues rather than work (substantive) issues. Enrico is attending night school to get his degree, but he comes to work late and spends time doing research instead of focusing on the job. The other team members have to pick up his slack. They can confront Enrico and demand his full participation, they can ignore him while tensions continue to grow, or they can complain to the manager. All the options will lower team performance.

Competition over resources, such as information, money, supplies or access to technology, can also cause conflict. Maria is supposed to have use of the laboratory in the afternoons, but Jason regularly overstays his allotted time, and Maria's work suffers. Maria might try to "get even" by denying Jason something he needs, such as information, or by complaining to other team members.

Communication breakdowns cause conflict—and misunderstandings are exacerbated in virtual teams and teams with cross-cultural members. The project manager should be precise in his expectations from all team members and be easily accessible. When members work independently, it is critical that they understand how their contributions affect the big picture in order to stay motivated. Carl couldn't understand why Latisha was angry with him when he was late with his reports—he didn't report to her. He didn't realize that she needed his data to complete her assignments. She eventually quit, and the team lost a good worker.

Team morale can be low because of external work conditions such as rumors of downsizing or fears that the competition is beating them to market. A manager needs to understand what external conditions are influencing team performance.

There are eight reasons for conflict, and they are:

Understanding the underlying reasons of conflict is essential to resolving it successfully. The following are some of the most typical causes of disagreement (Team Problem Solver).

Perceived breakdown of faith and trust: Individuals' faith and trust have been breached. There may be a rise in hostility when one person's faith and confidence in the other is shaken. As a result of a trusting connection, people feel more secure and confident in their lives. When trust is violated, our deepest emotions are unleashed, which often lead to confrontation..

Second, there are always going to be disputes. However, the accompanying sensations and emotions will persist to some degree if they are not resolved. This buried emotion can erupt with power when another situation brings this argument back to the forefront. Because of this, it is imperative that disagreements be resolved as soon as possible and not allowed to fester.

Our ability to communicate is one of our most frequently employed abilities. There are moments when our words fail to convey the picture we have in our minds. Errors and dissatisfaction are common outcomes when this occurs. If neither party is prepared to accept responsibility for the blunder, it might lead to conflict, depending on a variety of conditions (such as the level of stress present).

We're all unique individuals, and our personalities might clash. We are all born with a unique set of traits that we prefer to exhibit, according to experts.

There are many ways in which these innate distinctions contribute to our success as individuals and as teams.

Our values are the beliefs we possess that guide us in making decisions about what is right or wrong, good or bad, and normal or abnormal. As children, we learn about morality from our families, friends and mentors. We also learn about morality from the Bible and other religious texts. Because no two people have ever had the same life, we each have our own unique set of values and beliefs that influence the way we act and make decisions. Values are a powerful driver of conduct and a common source of conflict in our personal and professional lives.

Our lives today demand a great deal of our time and energy, which can lead to feelings of stress and anxiety. However, we are usually unable to meet these requests. In spite of this, we show up for work and try to function as normal as possible with our coworkers. At the least provocation, however, this underlying stress comes to the surface.

Human behavior and decisions are heavily influenced by our egos. When we feel like we're right, our egos get the better of us and we'll do anything to prove it. You can quickly defuse an argument or disagreement by admitting your mistakes. At the very least, try to put yourself in the other person's shoes and see things from their perspective.

Combinations of the aforementioned: Conflicts rarely have a single clear-cut cause.

In most cases, the elements stated are involved. Misunderstandings can give rise to misunderstandings, which can give rise to a quarrel.

Causes of Conflict II: Nine

Nine possible causes of conflict include: conflict with self, confrontation with others, disagreement with needs or wants, dispute with values, conflict with perceptions, conflict with assumptions, conflict with knowledge, conflict with expectations, conflict with personality, racial, or gender disparities (N.S.B.A., 2007).

CHAPTER SEVEN

Organizational Conflict

Definition: Organizational Conflict or otherwise known as workplace conflict, is described as the state of disagreement or misunderstanding, resulting from the actual or perceived dissent of needs, beliefs, resources and relationship between the members of the organization. At the workplace, whenever, two or more persons interact, conflict occurs when opinions with respect to any task or decision are in contradiction.

Individuals or groups inside an organization may disagree or misinterpret each other's needs, ideas, views, values, or goals, which is known as organizational conflict.

When two or more people interact in the workplace and their views on a job or decision diverge, conflict ensues.

An example of organizational conflict is when employees want to raise their wages, but management wants to keep them at the current levels.

Factors Affecting Conflict in the Workplace

If the responsibilities of various parts of a work or project aren't clearly defined, it might lead to conflict. To avoid this, the roles and responsibilities of the team members should be clearly defined and also agreed upon by all members of the team.

Conflicts in the workplace are frequently the result of interpersonal problems that exist among the people that make up the organization. The personalities of each member of an organization play a critical part in settling conflict in the workplace.

There are many factors that contribute to conflict in organizations, but one of the most common is a lack of resources, which causes individuals to compete with one another, which in turn leads to conflict.

This can lead to conflict of interest, as individuals may try to advance their own interests over the interests and aims of their employers, compromising the project's chances of completion.

Types of Conflict in the Workplace

First, there is inter-individual conflict.

Intra-personal conflict can occur when an individual's goals and visions conflict with the general goals and vision of the firm.

A person's internal dispute might be described as "intrapersonal." The person's mind is where the experience takes place. Since the dispute involves the mind and emotions of the individual, it can be classified as a psychological type of conflict.

Unwelcome visitors and phone calls can be avoided when a secretary lies that her boss is not present in the office. The secretary, who may have established an ethic of telling the truth, may have a problem with this.

A person may also be confronted with a role conflict in addition to these value conflicts. At his brother's wedding to his brother's police officer, he might find several of his family members utilizing illegal narcotics. It may drive him to question whether he should act as a police officer or as a brother.

2. Disputes between friends and family members

Conflict between two or more people in an organization is referred to as "interpersonal conflict."

As a result of individual variances, this occurs. It's common for people to have different personalities, which can lead to conflicting views and decisions. This could be a source of conflict between two managers who are vying for limited capital and labor.

Due to money and positional limits, if two equally deserving academics are both up for promotion but only one can be promoted, this could lead to interpersonal conflict between the two professors.

It's also possible that conflicts about the organization's aims and objectives can lead to conflict between employees. Some members of an organization's board may advocate for a "open admission" policy that would allow all high school graduates to be considered for admission to a college or university with a focus on excellent education. A situation like this can lead to disagreements among the members of the board of directors.

It is possible to have disagreements about the aims and objectives themselves, as well as about how to achieve them.

It's not uncommon for two marketing managers to disagree on the best promotional strategy for a company's products.

Conflict within a group

Individuals within a group come into conflict with one another. More than one individual may be involved in a group disagreement. Intragroup strife is the result of personality clashes and misunderstandings among the group's members. Team members may have diverse personalities and this can lead to tension or conflicts in their opinions and ideas.

All waiters and waitresses in some restaurants share in the tips equally. It's possible that a certain waitress, who's overly pleasant and efficient, believes she's entitled to more, resulting in tension with the group. It is also possible that some members of a group will be unable to participate in a strike because they disagree with the reasons for it or cannot afford to do so.

Conflict between groups is also referred to as inter-group conflict.

Because of a misunderstanding, intergroup conflict can happen in an organization.

This is because each of these groups has a separate set of goals and interests.

In addition, intergroup conflict is exacerbated by competitiveness. Other elements contribute to the escalation of hostilities. There may be a competition for resources or a group's borders that determine their identity as a team.

For example, commission-based salespeople may make promises to consumers about product quantities and delivery dates that the manufacturing department would be unable to match, resulting in a rift between the two departments.

Anxiety and Discord Among Organizations

This type of conflict occurs when individuals or groups inside one organization have disagreements with those in another. Inter-organizational conflict occurs when two or more organizations compete against each other.

Additionally, there is a lot of conflict between groups that are dependent on each other in some way. This may be a disagreement over raw material amount, quality, and delivery schedules, as well as other policy concerns, between purchaser and supplier groups.

Causes of conflict in the workplace

Every employee is expected to meet the goals imposed by his or her superior, and conflicts emerge when expectations are misunderstood or not met within the given timeframes.

Workplace conflict is often caused by communication breakdowns, such as when one employee needs certain information from another, but the other doesn't react in a timely manner.

It's also possible that misinterpretation of information, if one individual does it, can lead to a chain reaction of conflict in the workplace.

In a project when roles are not clearly defined and a mistake has occurred, which no member of the team wants to take blame, conflict might ensue.

A conflict goes through five stages.

It is possible for someone to be in conflict without being aware of it in the "Latent Step," the first stage in the five phases of conflict Servers in restaurants may submit orders erroneously, which may result in incorrect food being served to customers. Since neither the management nor the table are aware of this, there hasn't been any conflict.

People involved in a disagreement are now aware that there is a conflict, and management has been made aware of the situation through complaints. Management will now go over to the employee's location and have a conversation with them about it.

This stage is characterized by feelings of stress and anxiety on the part of one or more of the players. The boss doesn't love inciting discord, and the employee doesn't like to be the target of criticism.

This will surely lead to the "Manifest Stage," during which the conflict can be seen. E-mails, phone calls, phone texts, face-to-face meetings or any other situation where the disagreement can be viewed are all examples of the Manifest Stage. When a manager takes an employee out of the public eye to meet with him or her, the dispute is already on display.

The "Aftermath Stage," which occurs when the dispute is resolved or dissolving, is the final stage. When the manager takes steps to guarantee that the server is more cautious in the future and corrects the mistake with the customer.

Factors Influencing Organizational Conflict

Unclear Responsibility: If there is lack of clarity, regarding who is responsible for which section of a task or project, conflict takes place. And, to avoid this situation, the roles and responsibility of the team members should be stated clearly and also agreed upon by all.

Interpersonal Relationship: Every member of an organization, possesses different personality, which plays a crucial role in resolving conflict in an organization. Conflicts at the workplace, are often caused by interpersonal issues between the members of the organization.

Scarcity of Resources: One of the main reason for occurence of conflict in an organization is the inadequacy of resources like time, money, materials etc. due to which members of the organization compete with each other, leading to conflict between them.

Conflict of Interest: When there is a disorientation between the personal goals of the individual and the goals of the organization, conflict of interest arises, as the individual may fight for his personal goals, which hinders the overall success of the project.

Conflicts alleviate at the workplace due to individual and inter-individual factors. Individual related causes entails attitudes, beliefs, personality orientation and human-frailties. Inter-individual conflicts arises when a manager breaches norms of the organization.

Ways to Manage Conflicts in Organization

- Handle the conflict positively.
- Formation of official grievance procedure for all members.
- Concentrate on the causes rather than their effect, to assess conflicts.
- Parties to conflicts should be given an equal voice, irrespective of their position, term or political influence.
- Active participation of all the parties to conflict can also help to counter it.

In an organization, conflict is inevitable and so various means are to be discovered to resolve them or use them in a way that can help the organization to increase its productivity.

- Set up a formal grievances procedure that will listen to all the issues and take appropriate steps to find a viable solution
- All the involved parties must be given the necessary time to speak and lay their case
- Make sure that all conflicts are handled in a positive manner
- Try to concentrate on cause and not effect while finding a solution for resolving the organizational conflict

- Active participation and the desire to find a solution can pave the way for steps to manage and resolve the organizational conflict.

❧❧❧

❧❧❧

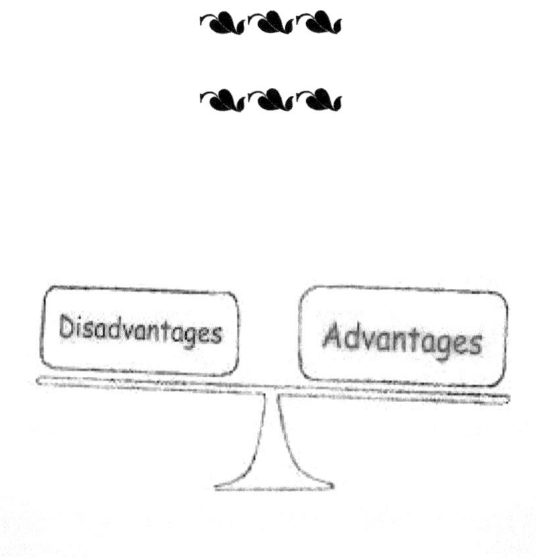

Advantages:

1. Encourages healthy argument

When there is a difference in opinion, it leads to organizational conflict. The best thing about it is that it results in debate and discussion along with healthy competition that can prove advantageous if you treat it positively.

It improves team culture and helps people to know about the viewpoint of other involved parties. This encourages team members to handle situations without losing their cool

2. Boost motivation

Friendly rivalry and debate can be a great motivational tool that helps productivity

3. Encourages to reach the set goals

It is a fact that when individuals are fighting it out amongst themselves about the best ways, then they are automatically moving towards their goals.

Dealing with difficult situations becomes easy as the debates and arguments offer various perspectives that can be used favourably.

4. Clarifies doubts and queries

Organizational conflicts help to clarify doubts. This ultimately improves the workplace environment

5. Sense of commitment

One of the advantages of organizational conflict is that it encourages a sense of commitment amongst team members.

6. Removes anxiety and stress

During conflicts, all the concerned parties are involved in arguments, and this proves cathartic as all your negative emotions are swept away. This ultimately reduces the levels of anxiety and stress and leads to a calm ad peaceful environment

7. Boosts productivity

Organizational conflict leads to resolution of issues that otherwise could have proved harmful. This ultimately is a reason for being more productive in future

8. Encourages change

Organizational conflict encourages change by helping you to find solutions to the existing issues.

9. Creating new ideas

During disagreements, it is possible to get hold of some intriguing ideas that can prove beneficial.

Disadvantages:

The disadvantages are as follows

1. Diverts attention from significant issues

Organizational conflicts often divert attention from the main problem as people keep on disagreeing and shifting topics to prove their point

2. Creating deadlocks

During the organizational conflict, people start putting their onus on differences and this results in a deadlock

3. Delaying decisions

Some individuals will rebel against working under others or even in teams under a team leader. They will keep on interfering in essential matters and ultimately become a reason for delaying decisions.

4. Leads to frustration

Organizational conflict does not allow individuals to listen to the argument of others. It leads to frustration, anxiety and disagreements that can continue for a long time and prove harmful for the company

5. Withholding information

In case of organizational conflict individuals, teams or even departments tend to withhold critical information that can slow down the completion of tasks

6. Reduces communication

When there is an ongoing conflict, people tend to become cynical and generally adopt either aggressive or avoidance behaviour. This often results in missed and reduced communication as no one is interested in talking then

CHAPTER EIGHT

Conflict Resolution

Conflict resolution is a way for two or more parties to find a peaceful solution to a disagreement among them. The disagreement may be personal, financial, political, or emotional. When a dispute arises, often the best course of action is negotiation to resolve the disagreement.

Team Conflict Resolution Methods

I. Levineís Resolution Model Drawing on his extensive experience, Levine (1998) shares a model for conflict resolution. The seven steps of his resolution model are discussed below:

1. Develop an Attitude of Resolution: The above process will not work unless one first holds certain values that make up an attitude of resolution. Levine discusses values such as believing in abundance, being creative, and relying on feelings and intuition.

2. Tell Your Story: Telling your story is listening to all stories, including yours. It is about understanding and being understood. Looking for ìthe truthî in their story is not as important as honoring their authenticity, and understanding ìtheir truth.

3. Listen for a Preliminary Vision of Resolution: Listening for a preliminary vision of resolution is thinking about a resolution that honors all concerns in the situation. It is about shifting from the desire to win, and get ones way, to a vision that everyone can buy into.

4. Get Current and Complete: Getting current and complete is saying what usually goes unsaid. It demands saying difficult, sometimes gut-wrenching things, thereby escaping from the emotional prisons that keep us locked in the past.

5. See a Vision for the Future: Seeing a vision for the future means reaching a general understanding of the resolution- a foundation of a new agreement. It requires letting go of the desire for what you know will not work and focuses on what will.

6. Craft the New Agreement: Crafting the new agreement adds the specifics. The key point is to have a map or formula for the dialogue that will maximize the potential for everyone to obtain his or her desired results.

7. Resolution: Resolution is moving back into action. With a new agreement, and a quiet, clear mind about the past, one can freely move forward.

II. McDanielís Team Mediation Process McDaniel et al. (1998) offer a step-by-step mediation process for teams dealing with conflict. This mediation process provides the work team with skills and structure for mediating their own disputes. Following are four requirements for effective implementation of this team mediation process.

1. Communication Skills: The first requirement is for each team member to be able to learn the appropriate communication skills and the overall mediation process. These communication skills include learning to confront others, listening to otherís concerns, acknowledging opposing perspectives,

responding appropriately, and committing to a plan of agreed action.

2. Individual Certification: The next requirement is the individual certification of competency for each memberís use of the mediation skills and understanding of the process. Competency ratings are used in other areas of skill, such as technical competencies, and are appropriate measures of interpersonal conflict skill usage.

3. Environment: The third requirement for effective mediation implementation is an environment in which the team is empowered to solve their own conflicts. The team must have the authority to create and establish its system of mediation. For example, the team begins to establish the system by brainstorming over the ideas of conflict, the negative results, and the positive outcomes for the team. Within this process, the team defines agreed upon team values, expectations, and procedures. This process is referred to as setting the path or boundaries of acceptable behavior for the team.

4. Collectivity: The team members are expected to recognize and resolve conflicts collectively. Team self-reliance for conflict resolution ranges from situations involving only two members, to complex situations, involving disagreement among all team members. The mediation process provides the team with the ability to handle conflict at both extremes.

III. Rayeski and Bryant Team Resolution Process Team Resolution Process is defined by Rayeski and Bryant (1994) as, ìthe process by which an individual, when provided an opportunity for improvement, accepts and makes a conscious, personal commitment to act upon this opportunity to enhance his/her performanceî.

Rayeski and Bryantís procedure includes the following three steps for addressing an escalating conflict:

1. Collaboration: Initially, as conflict arises, it should be handled informally between the twoteam members in a private setting. This method of collaboration provides the opportunity for selfcorrective behavior by the individual, without the need for any formal disciplinary action.

2. Mediation: The second step is mediation. If the situation escalates, a mediator is brought into the dispute to assist both sides in reaching an agreement. This mediation step is needed when an issue between individual members becomes disruptive to the team and collaboration attempts are ineffective. Efforts are made to relate the problem to customer and/or organizational needs. The success of this step relies on the neutrality of the mediator and the degree to which the team trusts this individual.

3. Team Counseling: The third step is team counseling. If efforts of collaboration and mediation fail, this is the final step for resolving an escalating team conflict situation. Team counseling is held at a team meeting, with all members of the team present. The issue is presented along with all the facts surrounding the disagreement.

IV. Wisinskiís Team Conflict Resolution Skills Once a person enters into a team membership, he or she is entering into an interdependent relationship. There is a sense that a person is giving up oneís individuality, yet the contribution to the team produces an end result greater than that achieved by individual effort.

Wisinski, (1995) proposes the use of the following six skills required for team membership to maintain strong team relationships needed for addressing conflict.

1. Participation: Participation indicates that a member is involved in the team in a balanced manner; the member is neither too withdrawn, nor overbearing or dominant. Each member is aware of this balance and helps others to maintain their respective balance.

2. Claiming: There is a need for individual members to claim their ideas. For example, when offering an alternative solution for a problem, the member is prepared ahead of time and provides the necessary perspective on what this means for the team as a whole. In addition, the member is able to defend his or her view with logic rather than emotion.

3. Relinquishing: Relinquishing is the ability of a team member presenting his or her personal opinion to withdraw it if it fails to gain the support of the team. The member relinquishes the position in favor of a direction agreed upon by the entire team.

4. Evaluating: Evaluating is the responsibility of each member to offer feedback stating any improvements or failures for the work of the team.

5. Healthy Environment: Relationships are detrimental to the process of managing conflict productively. Each member is responsible for maintaining supportive, healthy relationships within the team. There is a strong need placed on the individual to manage conflict between other team members.

6. Task Accomplishment: Task accomplishment is the responsibility of a team member to understand what items and tasks they are responsible for in a functioning team role. This includes knowing when tasks need to be completed and the steps involved to complete each task.

Seven Steps to Conflict Resolution:

The ability to resolve a conflict is a highly prized skill. Getting into conflict is easy, getting out of it is something else. The following Seven steps will give a direction on how to approach conflict (Team Problem Solver).

1. Develop an attitude of resolution: Take a deep breath and count to 10. Think about the conflict and what gave rise to it. Instead of seeing oneself as a victim, think about his/her own behavior. Try to change once mental state from one of anger and confrontation to one of calm, inquiry, and resolution.

2. Set the stage, plan your approach: After putting oneself in a better frame of mind (in step 1), it is now time to plan his/her approach to the resolution. If one is still angry, find a safe place and person with whom one can vent his/her anger and get some honest, objective feedback.

3. Arrange a place and time to talk: Choose a time and a place convenient to both parties where they can focus attention on resolution. Sometimes it is useful to find an environment different from the setting where the conflict arose. For example, one might suggest a walk outside or sit at a picnic table.

4. Tell your stories; gain an understanding of the issues: Covey (1994) in his book The Seven Habits of Highly Effective People says, ìseek first to understand, then to be understood. Ask the person to relate his/her side of the conflict. Then sit back, and listen. Ask questions, and seek to understand why they see it that way without implying they are wrong. Restate the key points and ask the person if you have heard them correctly. This is a critical step, because it will tend to defuse hostility. Then tell them your story, and ask them to suspend judgment until youíve finished. As these stories are being told, listen for a preliminary vision of resolution. There is a tendency to rush in and resolve conflict before we ever have a real understanding of the underlying issues. Telling your stories and really listening will provide a framework for this understanding.

5. Listen actively and with empathy: Active listening entails: looking directly at the person, making eye-to-eye contact, nodding occasionally (to indicate comprehension and agreement), sitting quietly, speaking only for clarification and summarizing their key points (to demonstrate comprehension). As a person tells his/her story and perceives he/she being heard, tension tends to decrease and real dialogue begins. Sometimes just the act of being heard is all that is necessary to defuse a conflict.

6. Generate solutions and a shared, win-win vision of resolution: A good, win-win solution comes from a sense of fairness. It honors that there are elements of truth in each personís story, and so the resolution should consider this. Brainstorm with the parties for ideas on how to resolve the

issue. Explore and be creative in searching alternatives.

7. Test for satisfaction: Ask each party if the solution works for them. This again involves actively listing to the response. If one party is not really satisfied with the outcome, but is not saying so, then the conflict will probably arise again. Finding satisfaction releases tension and hostility

CONFLICT RESOLUTION

Five Modes of Resolving Conflict

Conflict-Handling ModesAppropriate Situations

Source: Adapted from K. W. Thomas, “Toward Multidimensional Values in Teaching: The Example of Conflict Behaviors,” Academy of Management Review 2 (1977), Table 1, p. 487.

1. Competing

- When quick, decisive action is vital—e.g., emergencies
- On important issues where unpopular actions need implementing—e.g., cost cutting, enforcing unpopular rules, discipline

- On issues vital to company welfare when you know you're right
- Against people who take advantage of noncompetitive behavior

2. Collaborating

When trying to find an integrative solution when both sets of concerns are too important to be compromised

- When your objective is to learn
- When merging insights from people with different perspectives
- When gaining commitment by incorporating concerns into a consensus
- When working through feelings that have interfered with a relationship

3. Compromising

- When goals are important but not worth the effort or potential disruption of more assertive modes
- When opponents with equal power are committed to mutually exclusive goals
- When attempting to achieve temporary settlements to complex issues
- When arriving at expedient solutions under time pressure
- As a backup when collaboration or competition is unsuccessful

4. Avoiding

- When an issue is trivial, or when more important issues are pressing
- When you perceive no chance of satisfying your concerns
- When potential disruption outweighs the benefits of resolution
- When letting people cool down and regain perspective
- When gathering information supersedes immediate decision
- When others can resolve the conflict more effectively
- When issues seem tangential or symptomatic of other issues

5. Accommodating

- When you find you are wrong—to allow a better position to be heard, to learn, and to show your reasonableness
- When issues are more important to others than yourself—to satisfy others and maintain cooperation

- When building social credits for later issues
- When minimizing loss when you are outmatched and losing
- When harmony and stability are especially important.
- When allowing subordinates to develop by learning from mistakes.

Suggestions to resolve conflicts

Conflict is not a strange thing for people. Human beings experience it in their day-to-day lives – with their friends, families, and more so their professional lives. In the workplace, conflict causes a massive degree of frustration, pain, discomfort, sadness, as well as anger. It is a normal life aspect. In the world of today, organizations hire employees from diverse geographical locations with dissimilar cultural and intellectual backgrounds, as well as various viewpoints. In a working environment where people have disparate outlooks toward the same problems, disagreements are bound to happen.

Conflicts are inevitable in a person's day-to-day life. And when they happen, the idea is not to try to prevent them but rather to resolve and manage them in an effective manner. When people use the appropriate tools of resolution to address issues, they will be able to keep their differences from rising to major problems. "Establishing conflict management processes in a company is fundamental as it helps reduce conflict instances among employees," says Casper Hansen, an expert in resume writing from Resumethatworks. Conflict resolution is integral in the corporate world as it helps to distinguish a good business from a bad one. So, as a business owner, what steps should you follow to resolve a conflict? Well, below are some ways through which you can manage and resolve conflict in the workplace.

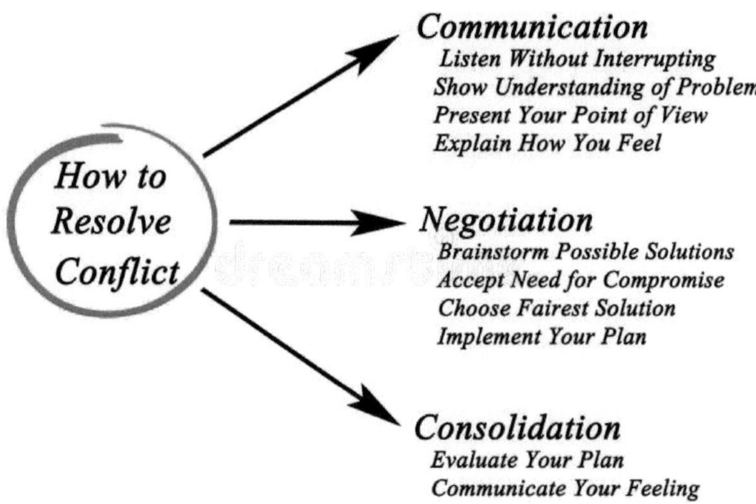

To manage conflict effectively you must be a skilled communicator. That includes creating an open communication environment in your unit by encouraging employees to talk about work issues. Listening to employee concerns will foster an open environment. Make sure you really understand what employees are saying by asking questions and focusing on their perception of the problem.

Whether you have two employees who are fighting for the desk next to the window or one employee who wants the heat on and another who doesn't, your immediate response to conflict situations is essential. Here are some tips you can use when faced with employees who can't resolve their own conflicts.

Acknowledge that a difficult situation exists. Honesty and clear communication play an important role in the resolution process. Acquaint yourself with what's happening and be open about the problem.

Let individuals express their feelings. Some feelings of anger and/or hurt usually accompany conflict situations. Before any kind of problem-solving can take place, these emotions should be expressed and acknowledged.

Define the problem. What is the stated problem? What is the negative impact on the work or relationships? Are differing personality styles part of the problem? Meet with employees separately at first and question them about the situation.

Determine underlying need. The goal of conflict resolution is not to decide which person is right or wrong; the goal is to reach a solution that everyone can live with. Looking first for needs, rather than solutions, is a powerful tool for generating win/win options. To discover needs, you must try to find out why people want the solutions they initially proposed. Once you understand the advantages their solutions have for them, you have discovered their needs.

Find common areas of agreement, no matter how small:

- Agree on the problem
- Agree on the procedure to follow
- Agree on worst fears
- Agree on some small change to give an experience of success
- Find solutions to satisfy needs:
- Problem-solve by generating multiple alternatives
- Determine which actions will be taken

Make sure involved parties buy into actions. (Total silence may be a sign of passive resistance.) Be sure you get real agreement from everyone.

Determine follow-up you will take to monitor actions. You may want to schedule a follow-up meeting in about two weeks to determine how the parties are doing.

Determine what you'll do if the conflict goes unresolved. If the conflict is causing a disruption in the department and it remains unresolved, you may need to explore other avenues.

Suggestions Following are the valuable suggestions to resolve conflicts (Team Problem Solver).

I. Training on the Human Dynamics of Working Together:

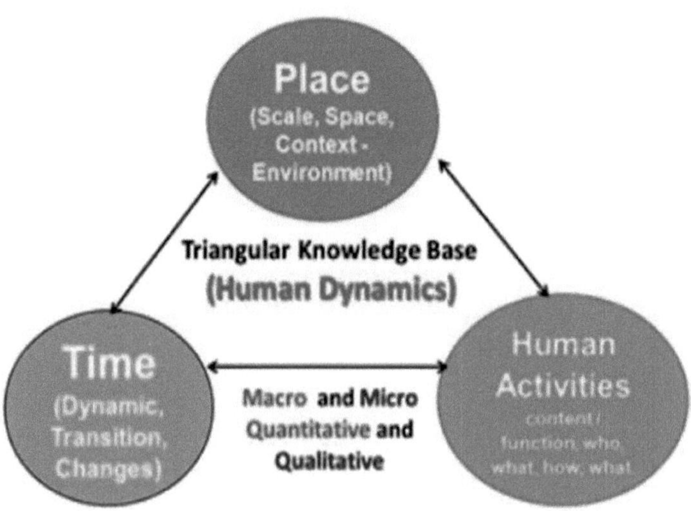

Get training on the human dynamics of working together on issues like how to deal with team conflict, how to minimize team conflict in the first place. Most teams are first taught how to do the work the task at hand. Secondarily they are taught the human dynamics of working together. As a result, when issues arise stemming from interpersonal relationships, team members may find themselves frustrated, in frequent disagreements, and conflict simply because they really do not understand each othersí unique personalities, beliefs, and ecentricities. As a first step in developing your new team, find someone who can teach team dynamics.

II. Gain Alignment Around Core Team Processes Create alignment around core team processes. The team should meet and discuss core team processes to create alignment on what they do and how they will operate. Some of these key processes include: the teamís mission, vision, and values, how decisions will be made, the roles and responsibilities of each team member, how work is assigned, how conflicts are resolved, how team members will be trained and developed. In general, any process that may hold the possibility of conflict should be discussed and agreed upon by all team members.

III. Develop a Conflict Resolution Process One of the simplest, but best, ways to deal with team conflict is to develop a resolution process at the outset. Talk openly with team members about the inevitability of conflict and how they would like to deal with it. The process can vary from team to team, so have them develop their own process that each member agrees to abide by. When conflicts arise, use the process.

IV. Keep Disagreement from Escalating into Conflict Members should openly discuss the importance of disagreement. Without disagreement, teams can fall into groupthink, or a tendency to blindly agree on issues without proper questioning. Team members sometimes fall into this trap to avoid conflict, but then fall into a larger one of making poor decisions. So disagreement and good argumentative discussion should be encouraged. However, team members should also discuss when this disagreement crosses the line into open conflict that may be harmful to the team. Having a discussion about disagreement and conflict is an adult behavior. And team members will appreciate the opportunity to have this discussion and resolve in advance what could be a barrier to higher team performance.

V. Dealings with Difficult Team Members The first step to deal with difficult team member is to develop a relationship or friendship that provides safety and security. As this relationship develops, the person will become more receptive to feedback and more likely to experience a ìturnaroundî in their behavior. This approach requires one to move to a higher plane of thinking, one that understands that more can be accomplished through unselfish service to others rather than retreating to the comfort of our own egos and insecurities. VI. Focused Feedback and Follow-up Focused feedback and follow-up increase leadership and customer service effectiveness. Team members must have the courage to ask regularly for feedback and the discipline to develop a behavioral change strategy, to follow-up, and to stick with it. Greater teamwork occurs when team members develop their own behavioral change strategy, as opposed to having one imposed on them (Goldsmith and Morgan 2006).

VI. Involve the Team Leader Where team members are unable to resolve their differences, it may be necessary to involve the team leader. The strategy here should be for the team leader to give each person the opportunity to state his or her feelings about the issue. Once the feelings of both sides have been expressed, the facts of the case can be dealt with (West, 1996).

VII. Build a Good Team

- There should be a high level of interdependence among team members.
- Each member needs to realize that he or she cannot progress unless the team does well.
- A team needs a leader who is very committed, and an outstanding communicator.
- Each team member needs to be willing to contribute his or her best efforts.
- A certain degree of camaraderie fosters the effectiveness of the team.
- Team members need to enjoy each otherís company, laugh together, and have fun while working.
- Team building depends on the mutual trust and respect that members develop for each other.

- Disagreements between team members have to be resolved in a mature manner, without resolving to personal attacks (Deshpande, 2007).

End Note

Disagreements are common in the workplace and should be expected at some point during the company's existence. Maintaining a positive outlook is critical when confronted with these problems. Internal organizational disputes can be good or damaging; nonetheless, beneficial conflicts can motivate you to work harder and more efficiently. Management must address disagreements that are harmful to the organization so that they do not depress the morale of other employees and harm the ambience.

Workplace conflict exists between individuals and groups, it may lead to a series of negative influence to the organization. When people work together, cultural differences, gender differences, style differences, all kinds of differences occur. Resolve and avoid the conflict in workplace may increase effectiveness for work. Effectively managed work conflict has many positive results for the organization even our life.

9 798887 046501

Printed by Libri Plureos GmbH in Hamburg,
Germany